Chocolates on the Pillow

GAIL GRECO'S
LITTLE
Bed & Breakfast
COOKBOOK SERIES

Chocolates on the Pillow

Text by GAIL GRECO

Photographs by TOM BAGLEY

RUTLEDGE HILL PRESS
Nashville, Tennessee

Published in Nashville, Tennessee, by Rutledge Hill Press, Inc., 211 Seventh Avenue North, Nashville, Tennessee 37219. Distributed in Canada by H.B. Fenn & Company, Ltd., 34 Nixon Road, Bolton, Ontario L7E 1W2. Distributed in Australia by Millennium Books, 33 Maddox Street, Alexandria NSW 2015. Distributed in New Zealand by Tandem Press, 2 Rugby Road, Birkenhead, Auckland 10. Distributed in the United Kingdom by Verulam Publishing, Ltd., 152a Park Street Lane, Park Street, St. Albans, Hertfordshire AL2 2AU.

Photographs by Tom Bagley

Photo art direction and styling by Gail Greco

Food preparation assistance by Ceilia St. Onge, Yvonne Martin, Priscilla Powers, and Sharon Burdick

Editorial assistance by Tricia Conaty

Cover and book design by Gore Studio, Inc.

Text layout and typesetting by John Wilson Design

All recipes selected and edited for the home kitchen by Gail Greco

ON THE FRONT COVER: CHOCOLATE BISCOTTI AT GINGERBREAD MANSION INN, FERNDALE, CALIFORNIA, RECIPE ON PAGE 34

Greco, Gail
    Chocolates on the pillow/ Gail Greco: photographs by Tom Bagley.
       p. cm.
    Includes index.
    ISBN 1-55853-454-7
    1. Cookery (Chocolate) 2. Desserts 3.Chocolate. I. Title.
    TX767.C5G744   1996
    641.6'374--dc20

Printed in the United States of America

1 2 3 4 5 6 7 8 9 — 00 99 98 97 96

*For the innkeepers. They offer
personal hospitality every
day in homelike settings.
Chocolates on the pillow are only
one small example of their
genuine pampering spirit.*

Contents

About the Recipe Test Kitchen   ix

INTRODUCTION: xi

MIDDAY MELTDOWN
29

Caramel Apple-and-Oat Squares

*Orange Chocolate Biscotti
with Chocolate Glaze*

Chocolate Carrot Bread

Fudge Pie

Peanut Butter Pie with Chocolate Glaze

Black Forest Cobbler

Marbled Chocolate Fruits

Orange-Walnut Chocolate Tart

Mocha Squares with Coffee Sauce

Old-Fashioned Fudge Cake with Walnuts

*Cream-Filled Chocolate and Raspberry
Cupcakes*

*Raspberry Cream Puffs with
Chocolate Ganache*

RISE 'N' BONBON
1

Chocolate and Strawberry Crêpes

Chocolate Waffles with Cherry Sauce

Sourdough Pain au Chocolat

*Cocoa-Nut Bread with
Chocolate Honey Butter*

Black Jack Muffins

Bran Muffins with Chocolate Filling

*Chocolate Pecan Bread with
Bourbon-Streusel Topping*

Chocolate Honey Soufflé

Chocolate Mint Breakfast Chews

EVENING EXPRESSIONS
61

Peppermint Parfaits with Chocolate Sauce

Iced Chocolate Cappuccino

Raspberry-Almond Pâté

Peanut Butter and Chocolate
Strawberry Fondue

Crème de Mocha Custard Pots

White-Chocolate Fettuccine with
Strawberry Sauce

Chocolate-Truffle Cheesecake with
Raspberry Sauce

Cocoa Kahlua Cake with Chocolate Glaze

Flourless Chocolate Cake with
Fruit Purée

Mocha Bourbon Pound Cake with Cream
Cheese Icing and Fresh Blackberries

SUITE DREAMS

83

Mini-Devil Cheesecakes

Chocolate-Raspberry Cordials

Chocolate Mudslide Drink

Kissed by a Bonbon

Chocolate-Dipped Maplenut Creams

Mints on the Pillow

Kahlua Chocolate Truffles

Chocolate Bavarian

Chocolate Jammin' Tassies

Inn Directory   103

Index   110

Other Books in This Series

✺

Vive la French Toast!
Autumn at the Farmers Market
Recipes for Romance

The Test Kitchen for the Cooking Association of Country Inns

Although all inn recipes are tried-and-true and served at the inns all the time, the recipes in this cookbook have been further verified and tested for accuracy and clarification for the home kitchen.

The cooking seal of approval that accompanies this book means that every recipe has been tested in kitchens other than the source, and that the association test kitchen has been satisfied that the recipe is proven and worthy of preparing.

The test kitchen is under the leadership of association founder Gail Greco, with Charla Honea and other editors at Rutledge Hill Press assisting. The prestigious list of kitchen testers is as follows:

∽o∾

DAVID CAMPICHE, *Chef/Owner*
The Shelburne Inn • Seaview, Washington

YVONNE MARTIN, *Chef/Owner*
The White Oak Inn • Danville, Ohio

DEBBIE MOSSIMAN, *Chef/Owner*
Swiss Woods • Lititz, Pennsylvania

PATRICK RUNKEL, *Chef/Owner*
October Country Inn • Bridgewater Corners, Vermont

LAURA SIMOES, *Chef/Owner*
The Inn at Maplewood Farm • Hillsborough, New Hampshire

ELIZABETH TURNEY, *Chef/Owner*
Bear Creek Lodge • Victor, Montana

MARION YADON, *Chef/Owner*
Canyon Villa Bed & Breakfast • Sedona, Arizona

CHOCOLATE PAIRS WELL WITH THE DUTCH-COCOA LOOK OF BLUE-AND-WHITE DELFT-STYLE PIECES FROM MY AUNT JO'S COLLECTION.

Chocolate Chips

GROWING UP IN THE 1950s and 1960s, I was surrounded by life's little pleasures and never even knew it. One of them was going grocery shopping every Friday night. Mom made it worth our while to help her with the task of shopping for six. Dad, who commuted two hours a day into New York City, found pleasure in staying at home, sitting down to a night of black-and-white television. (We couldn't afford the new color sets.) When we came home, Dad expected to find, in at least one of fifteen or so brown grocery bags, the snacks he had added to the shopping list.

I was the oldest, so Mom and I (and usually one of my toddler siblings) hopped into the station wagon and rode off to the supermarket. For me, it was a treat looking at all of the food products. I liked to eat, probably because my mother was an excellent cook, so almost everything appealed to me. But the real fun of the shopping excursion was in the snacks aisle. We were big on the new cheese pretzels from Nabisco and so was Dad, so we picked those up for him, knowing we would eat them that night in front of the television while Fred Flintstone figured out how to get him-

self out of another jam à la *I Love Lucy* or *My Little Margie*.

Mom often added spearmint-leaf gumdrops to the shopping cart, and we all agreed on one must-buy—a large bar of chocolate. We tried them all from Hershey's to Nestlé's Crunch and later Cadbury, filled with raisins. Sometimes we stocked up on the chocolate bars if Mom had a little more in the budget that week. Some of us preferred plain chocolate; others wanted chocolate with almonds.

Chocolate. Back then it was unadulterated pleasure with little concern for calories or fat. So every time our family got together with my aunt and uncle, I was delighted, because there would be a chocolate treat coming over as well. Aunt Jo and Uncle Tony always brought in the sweets, and Mom would make the coffee, a task that never intimidated her even though my uncle was a coffee connoisseur and salesman. She strived to do her best; impressing someone was never her measure for success. My aunt and uncle never worried about how their sweets would go over. They did their best, too. And one item in particular was a hit time after time. To this day, Ebinger's Blackout Cake in the

CHOCOLATES ON THE PILLOW AT PINEHILL B&B

striped baker's box remains my all-time favorite chocolate dessert.

The cake would arrive in a square box tied with several wraps of brown-and-green striped string to match the colors of the box. My aunt would set the cake on the table, and I would stare at the box, visualizing what was inside and how it got there. I would go back to its point-of-sale, seeing the cake in the glass case, hand-selected by my aunt. I could see the baker folding the flat cardboard cutout into a box, plopping the cake inside, and then pulling the string from some carefully contrived and mounted spool, using a sharp edge worn on the finger to snap the desired length from the bolt and fasten the box securely. The baker must have known this little bundle had to make an hour's drive from Brooklyn to another city borough. When my aunt pulled up to our driveway, wearing her Sunday best, topped by a proper two-pronged, flat but gently curved black vogue satin skull hat, she would grab the box containing the

Blackout Cake with her white-gloved hands and carry it ever so proudly.

There was no need to imagine the cake's scent. The chocolate was strong and intoxicating. Once the box was opened, the cake stood regally. It was incredibly black. About eight inches in diameter, the Blackout Cake was coated with cakelike soft shavings of black chocolate. A glossy dark-chocolate ganache would shine through the chocolate shavings as it caught light. Beyond the smooth and glossy ganache were layers of more chocolate. I sat at the table, eager but trying to be polite, waiting for the cake to be cut and hoping I would be served the first slice. With a glass of milk, there was no greater treat in the world to a kid growing up in a row house in the Bronx.

Aunt Jo's Blackout Cake became her signature. Nothing has duplicated that cake. Actually, the reason is because it was indeed an excellent and unusual cake from a very reputable bakery, but also I don't want anything to eclipse this fond memory of me and chocolate.

As I lie here chewing a chocolate on my pillow at Twin Gates Bed-and-Breakfast in Lutherville, Maryland, I am reminded about many "chocolate chips" or nougats of chocolate memories I have, many of them from the inns.

Inns are famous for their chocolates on the pillow, and I have eaten many as I have traveled around the country. As the B&B movement began spreading, travel writers touted this amenity as one of the main features that separated small inns from hotel chains—until the chains embraced the idea. I remember a note on my pillow at a major hotel in the early 1990s; it was the epitome of why these chains can never compete with the graciousness of small inns. The printed note said I could dial such-and-such a number to request turndown service and chocolates for my pillow. Humph!

Originally, chocolates on the pillow meant little evening snacks, cordials, or truffles that said good night from the innkeeper. But chocolates on the pillow mean much more. Some inns serve chocolate desserts by the bedside or have chocolate drinks awaiting guests' return from an evening on the town. Still others serve chocolate on breakfast trays in the form of muffins or waffles for morning versions of chocolates on the pillow.

This book is dedicated to the idea of chocolates on the pillow and how they serve to pamper and also to what serving chocolate any time of day will do for your own family and friends, who will then be able to turn these chocolate morsels or chocolate chips into their own sweet memories.

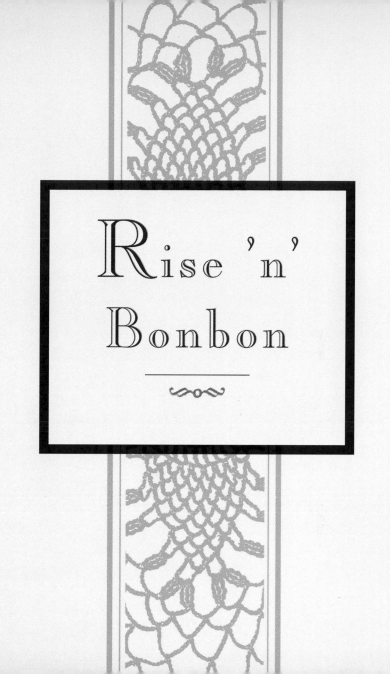

Rise 'n' Bonbon

Chocolate and Strawberry Crêpes

Crêpes are full of romantic traditions, and in Brittany, people make them everywhere, even on street corners. While this recipe will fill 10 crêpes, you will have extra batter to make double and freeze. The filling is for 10 crêpes. Be sure that the batter is spread thinly into the pan.

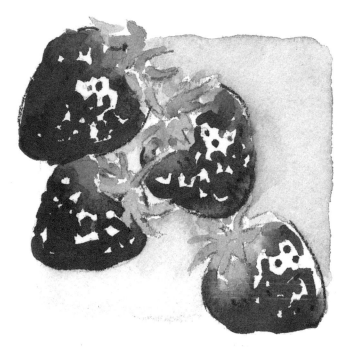

PICTURE FACING CHAPTER OPENER: SOURDOUGH PAIN AU CHOCOLAT AT THE INN AT MAPLEWOOD FARM, RECIPE ON PAGE 8

LEFT: A CAMBRIDGE HOUSE B&B

American Chocolate Week is the third week in March.

Chocolate and Strawberry Crêpes (continued)

Crêpes		Filling	
1	cup all-purpose flour	3	quarts strawberries, sliced (saving a few for garnish)
1/8	teaspoon salt		
3	eggs	2	tablespoons sugar
2	tablespoons butter, melted	2	cups heavy cream
1	cup plus 2 tablespoons milk	7	ounces quality sweet chocolate, grated
1	tablespoon clarified butter		

MAKES 10 SERVINGS

*P*repare the crêpes by sifting together the flour and salt into a large mixing bowl. Create a well in the center and break in the eggs. Slowly whisk the eggs into the flour until thoroughly incorporated. Stir in the melted butter. Then pour in the milk, a little at a time, whisking after each addition. When smooth, pour the batter through a mesh strainer into a clean bowl.

To cook, heat 1 to 2 tablespoons of the clarified butter in a crêpe pan set over medium-high heat. (Use a skillet with a 6-inch bottom if you do not have a crêpe pan.) Add just enough batter to coat the bottom of the pan. Heat until the crêpe is set and a light golden brown. Loosen the edges with a spatula and flip or turn. Brown the reverse side for just a few seconds. Set the crêpes aside to cool.

Prepare the filling. Toss the strawberry slices with the sugar. Whip the heavy cream until fluffy.

Place a spoonful each of strawberry slices, grated chocolate, and whipped cream in the center of each pancake. Fold the crêpe over to hold in the filling. Garnish with strawberry slices and the chocolate sauce.

—CAMBRIDGE HOUSE

Chocolate Waffles with Cherry Sauce

༺०༻

The cherry sauce nestles quietly into the nooks and crannies of the chocolate waffles. The chocolate chips spread flavor into every bite.

Sauce

- 2 cups pitted fresh Bing cherries (or 1/2 cup dried)
- 1 cup water
- 1/4 cup sugar
- 2 tablespoons cornstarch

Waffles

- 1 cup whole wheat flour
- 1 cup all-purpose flour
- 1 tablespoon sugar
- 2 teaspoons baking powder
- 1 teaspoon baking soda
- 1/8 teaspoon salt
- 3 eggs, separated
- 2 cups buttermilk
- 1/2 cup (1 stick) butter, melted
- 1/2 cup mini-chocolate chips

MAKES 6 SERVINGS

Prepare the sauce first. In a medium saucepan, over medium heat, cook the cherries in the water until softened. Add the sugar. Dissolve the cornstarch in a tablespoon or so of water. Add to the cherries and boil, stirring constantly, until the sauce has thickened. Remove from heat. Prepare the waffle batter.

In a large bowl, sift together the dry ingredients. In another large bowl, blend the egg yolks with the buttermilk and melted butter. Add the dry ingredients to the wet ingredients and mix just until moistened. Set aside.

In a separate bowl, beat the egg whites until peaks begin to form. Fold into the batter along with the chocolate chips. Bake in a hot waffle iron. Serve with the sauce.

—GAIL'S KITCHEN

Sourdough Pain au Chocolat

∽o∾

Bread and chocolate seem to go so well together. Why, there is even a small café chain by that name. This dish is simple to make and provides a surprising side dish for breakfast, with the sourdough as a nice accent to the sweet chocolate.

This inn is a delightful old farmhouse with a 1940s atmosphere. A herd of dairy cows nearby offers a chorus of melody as their Swiss cowbells tinkle easily with every bite of grass.

2	3-inch-thick slices sourdough French bread
2	tablespoons butter, softened
2	1-ounce squares semisweet chocolate
	Fresh mint leaves and raspberries, for garnish

MAKES 2 SERVINGS

Create pockets in the bread by slicing through the crust, being careful not to slice all the way through. Spread the outside of the bread with butter. Tuck a chocolate square into each pocket. If necessary, cut the square in half for a better fit. Place the stuffed bread slices on a hot skillet or griddle. Cook until the bread is browned on the outside and the chocolate has melted. Garnish and serve warm.

—INN AT MAPLEWOOD FARM

To make this easy Chocolate Breakfast Taco from Blue Harbor House, mix together ²/₃ cup all-purpose flour, ¹/₃ cup sugar, 1 teaspoon unsweetened cocoa. Add 1 egg, 1 egg white, ¹/₄ cup vegetable oil, and ¹/₄ cup skim milk, stirring until batter is smooth and creamy. Cover and refrigerate 2 hours until batter settles. Pour ¹/₄ cup batter into prepared crêpe pan and cook both over medium heat. Cool crêpes on rack and fill with fruits in season and edible flowers.

Cocoa-Nut Bread with Chocolate Honey Butter

⊷⊷

The delicious honey butter only enhances this fabulous bread. Make extra butter and slather it over English muffins when the bread runs out.

MANOR HOUSE
INN, CAPE MAY,
NEW JERSEY

Bread			****	½	teaspoon salt
1	cup sugar			½	teaspoon baking soda
½	cup (1 stick) butter			⅓	cup chopped nuts of choice
2	eggs		**Butter**		
1	cup buttermilk			½	cup butter
1 ¾	cups all-purpose flour			2	tablespoons honey
½	cup unsweetened cocoa powder			2	tablespoons chocolate syrup
½	teaspoon baking powder				

MAKES 1 LOAF

*P*reheat the oven to 350°. Begin by preparing the bread batter. In a large mixing bowl, cream together the sugar and butter. When smooth, add the eggs and mix well. Stir in the buttermilk. Add the flour, cocoa, baking powder, salt, and baking soda. Stir until the dry ingredients are just moistened. Stir in the nuts.

Pour the batter into a greased 9x5-inch loaf pan. Bake for 1 hour or until a tester comes clean. Remove the bread from the pan and let cool.

Prepare the honey butter. Combine the butter, honey, and chocolate syrup in a mixing bowl. Beat at high speed until the mixture is light and fluffy. Serve with slices of cocoa-nut bread.

—MANOR HOUSE INN

If you really want to plan your guests' weekend with an energized start, serve them your favorite homemade fudge. The folks at Florida House Inn on Amelia Island, Florida, stand by their most popular amenity—Old-Timey Fudge. The inn's fudge is homemade and left in the rooms for check-in time. The innkeepers have noticed the fudge is often eaten as soon as the guests check in.

Black Jack Muffins

A jambalaya of corn, black beans, cheese, and chocolate chips offers up a riotous flavor for breakfast.

2 ½	cups all-purpose flour
1 ½	cups cornmeal
4	teaspoons baking powder
1	teaspoon baking soda
1 ½	cups assorted shredded cheeses (sharp Cheddar, Monterey Jack, or jalapeño cheese)
2	tablespoons sugar
2	tablespoons chopped fresh cilantro

1	cup fresh corn kernels
¼	cup diced jalapeño peppers
½	cup cooked black beans, drained
¼	cup semisweet mini-chocolate chips
2	eggs
2	cups milk
½	cup melted butter, cooled slightly

MAKES 24 MUFFINS

Preheat the oven to 350°. In a large mixing bowl, combine the flour, cornmeal, baking powder, baking soda, cheese, sugar, cilantro, corn, peppers, black beans, and chocolate chips. Mix well. Add the eggs, milk, and butter, stirring until well blended.

Spoon the batter into lightly greased muffin tins, ⅔-full. Bake for 35 minutes or until springy to the touch and no longer moist in the center.

—PINEHILL B&B

RIGHT: BLACK JACK MUFFINS AND THE ENTRYWAY TO PINEHILL B&B

Bran Muffins with Chocolate Filling

⚬❀⚬

Bran muffins never had it so good before the addition of chocolate chips and cream cheese.

While munching on some chocolates left on your pillow, consider pleasant ideas such as this one before turning out the light: "A man is happy so long as he chooses to be happy and nothing else can stop him." Aleksandr Solzhenitsyn

Filling

2	cups semisweet chocolate chips
1	8-ounce package cream cheese, softened
1/4	cup sugar
2	tablespoons, plus 1 cup milk

Batter

2 1/2	cups all-purpose flour
1/2	cup firmly packed brown sugar

1	teaspoon baking soda
1	teaspoon baking powder
3/4	cup (1 1/2 sticks) butter
1/2	cup crushed all-bran cereal
2	eggs, slightly beaten
1	teaspoon vanilla extract

MAKES 12 MUFFINS

*P*reheat the oven to 350°. Melt the chocolate chips in a microwave or double boiler. Set aside to cool. Cream together the cream cheese, sugar, 2 tablespoons of the milk, and the melted chocolate until smooth and well blended.

In a separate bowl, combine the flour, brown sugar, baking soda, and baking powder. Cut in the butter, and mix well until crumbs form.

In another bowl, combine the cereal and the remaining 1 cup of milk. Let stand for about 5 minutes or until the cereal softens. Stir in the eggs and the vanilla. Pour the bran mixture into the bowl with the dry ingredients and stir until moist. Lightly coat a muffin tin with cooking oil spray and scoop the batter into 12 muffin cups, filling each halfway. Pour the chocolate mixture over the bran batter, dividing evenly among the muffin tins. Finish with another layer of the batter. Bake 15 to 20 minutes or until the tops spring back when touched.

—MAPLEWOOD INN

LEFT: CHOCOLATE EVEN MAKES IT INTO MORNING OATMEAL AT PINEHILL B&B. ADD CHOCOLATE CHIPS TO YOUR OWN OATMEAL RECIPE ALONG WITH SUNDRIED CRANBERRIES, CHOPPED WALNUTS, AND DRIED CHOPPED APPLES.

Chocolate Pecan Bread with Bourbon-Streusel Topping

∽◦∾

Sampson Eagon Inn also suggests that you may make this recipe in the form of muffins. Instead of using loaf pans, pour the batter evenly into twelve large, greased or nonstick muffin tins. Turn the cooking time down to about 30 minutes or until tester is clean. I enjoy this gracious inn on a quiet street in the little town of Staunton, Virginia.

LEFT: A RISE 'N' BONBON MORNING AT SAMPSON EAGON HOUSE INCLUDES A POACHED PEAR WITH CHOCOLATE SAUCE.

SAMPSON EAGON INN, STAUNTON, VIRGINIA

American food critics John and Karen Hess have an excuse for indulging in one last thing before getting under the covers: "The real American pattern of feeding is the snack. It lasts from early morning to bedtime." (The Cook's Notebook, Running Press.)

Chocolate Pecan Bread with Bourbon-Streusel Topping (continued)

Topping

1/4	cup coarsely chopped, toasted pecans
1/4	cup firmly packed brown sugar
3 1/2	tablespoons all-purpose flour
1 1/2	tablespoons butter, melted
2	teaspoons bourbon

Bread

3	cups all-purpose flour
1	cup sugar
2	teaspoons salt
4	teaspoons baking powder
4	tablespoons cold unsalted butter, cut into pieces
1 1/2	cups coarsely chopped toasted pecans
1	cup milk, room temperature
1	egg
1/2	cup bourbon
6	ounces chocolate chips

MAKES 4 MINI-LOAVES

*P*repare the topping in a medium bowl, combining the pecans, brown sugar, flour, butter, and bourbon. Set aside.

Preheat the oven to 400°. In a large bowl, combine the flour, sugar, salt, and baking powder. Cut in the butter with a pastry blender or fork, until the mixture forms coarse crumbs. Stir in the 1 1/2 cups of pecans. In a separate bowl, mix together the milk, egg, and the bourbon. Add this mixture to the flour-and-nuts mixture, stirring just to combine. Fold in the chocolate chips. Pour into 4 nonstick mini-bread pans. Evenly spread the streusel topping over the batter. Place the loaves in the oven and bake for about 1 hour or until a tester comes clean.

—THE SAMPSON EAGON INN

Chocolate Honey Soufflé

I love a soufflé, and for breakfast it is even more delightful. What an inflated way to start the day!

THE INN AT BUCKEYSTOWN, BUCKEYSTOWN, MARYLAND

4	eggs
1/2	cup honey, plus extra for garnish
1/2	cup chocolate syrup, plus extra for garnish
2 1/2	cups milk
3/4	teaspoon salt
1	cup all-purpose flour
4	tablespoons butter

MAKES 4 TO 6 SERVINGS

Preheat the oven to 425°. Place a 10 1/2 x 3-inch round baking dish in the oven for 10 minutes to warm.

In a mixing bowl, combine the eggs, honey, chocolate syrup, milk, and salt. Beat well with an electric mixer. Add the flour and beat until smooth.

Remove the baking dish from the oven and add the butter. When the butter has melted, pour in the chocolate-honey batter. Bake for 25 minutes or until golden brown. Drizzle with additional chocolate syrup and honey. The soufflé deflates rapidly—so serve immediately.

—THE INN AT BUCKEYSTOWN

Chef John Schumacher has a nice way to gourmandise homemade brownies. He adds currant jelly and a little brandy to the batter at his Schumacher's New Prague Hotel in New Prague, Minnesota.

Chocolate Mint Breakfast Chews

〜〜〜

Chef and innkeeper Dan Pelz adds these to the breakfast table to give folks a conversation piece and a surprise. I had a tough time deciding if these shouldn't also go in the Suite Dreams chapter for bedside. You decide.

2	(1-ounce) squares semisweet chocolate
$1/2$	cup (1 stick) butter, softened
1	cup sugar
2	eggs, lightly beaten
1	teaspoon vanilla extract
$3/4$	cup all-purpose flour
1	cup chopped walnuts
$1/2$	cup mint jelly
	Powdered sugar for garnish

Preheat the oven to 350°. Melt the chocolate in a small saucepan over low heat. Set aside to cool. Cream the butter in a large mixing bowl. When smooth, add the sugar, eggs, vanilla, flour, and melted chocolate. Stir well to combine. Gently fold in the walnuts. Pour the batter into an 8x11-inch nonstick baking pan. Spread the mint jelly evenly overtop, lightly pushing into the batter. Bake for 30 minutes. Cool and cut into 2-inch squares. Dust with powdered sugar.

—THE INN AT BUCKEYSTOWN

Chocolate in a main course? Yes, at The Inn at Maplewood Farm. Innkeeper Laura Simoes includes it in a platter of shrimp and scallops sautéed in butter, shallots, and garlic, then flambéed with cognac, semisweet chocolate, and grated chocolate garnish. How sweet it is. I'm sure Laura would give out the recipe if you write to her or visit the inn. Actually, chocolate in savory cooking was common during the time of the Aztecs, and one of the great dishes of Mexican cookery is still the mole poblano de guajolote (a turkey stew of unsweetened chocolate, flavored with chili peppers and sesame).

Midday Meltdown

Caramel Apple-and-Oat Squares

〜o〜

Breakfast at Pinehill always includes a few chocolate dishes. This recipe with its oats and apples seems well-suited for breakfast the Pinehill B&B way. Serve these squares as you would a side of muffins. They can really be cut any size and stretched as far as you would like. The recipe calls for the soft caramels in the cellophane wrappers—like the good old days. (Innkeeper Sharon Burdick founded what is believed to be the only B&B chocolate trail. Guests go from inn to inn sampling chocolate. Call Sharon at 815-732-2061 for a brochure on the Blackhawk Chocolate Trail.)

Picture facing Chapter Opener: An afternoon snack at Pinehill B&B, recipe above

Left: Pinehill B&B in Oregon, Illinois

Chocolate desserts are the cook's savior. When in doubt about what type of dessert to make for company, choose chocolate. Usually no one is disappointed.

Caramel Apple-and-Oat Squares (continued)

Crust		
1	cup lightly packed brown sugar	
1	cup (2 sticks) butter, cold	
2	cups all-purpose flour	
1/2	cup old-fashioned rolled oats	

Filling		
4	Granny Smith apples, peeled, cored, and thinly sliced	
2	tablespoons all-purpose flour	
1	teaspoon cinnamon	
20	caramel candies	
1	tablespoon water	
1/2	cup coarsely chopped pecans	
1/3	cup semisweet chocolate chips	

MAKES 18 SERVINGS

Preheat the oven to 325°. Prepare the crust. Combine the brown sugar, butter, and flour in a large bowl. Mix until the ingredients form coarse crumbs. Stir in the oats. Measure 1 cup of the crust mixture and set aside for later when preparing the topping.

Press the crust crumbs into a 9x13-inch greased baking dish. Arrange the apple slices over the crust, in symmetric rows. Sprinkle with the flour and cinnamon.

In a large saucepan, combine the caramels and water. Stir over medium-high heat until the caramels have melted. Pour the warm caramel mixture over the apples, distributing evenly. Sprinkle the pecans and chocolate chips over the top. Finish with a layer of the reserved crust crumbs.

Bake for 55 minutes or until chocolate is melted and mix is solidified. Let cool and cut into 2x3-inch or desired squares.

—PINEHILL B&B

Orange Chocolate Biscotti
with Chocolate Glaze

∞

Biscotti are hard Italian biscuits—great for dunking in a mug full of coffee, and it's perfectly acceptable. This recipe is loaded with chocolate.

3	cups all-purpose flour	1/3	cup olive oil
3/4	cup sugar	2	tablespoons orange juice
1/2	cup firmly packed brown sugar	2	tablespoons light or dark rum
1	tablespoon baking powder	1	tablespoon grated orange peel
3/4	teaspoon salt	1	teaspoon vanilla extract
3	ounces unsweetened baking chocolate, melted and cooled	1	cup semisweet chocolate chips
		1	cup chopped almonds
3	eggs	12	ounces white chocolate

MAKES 6 SERVINGS

In a large bowl, combine the flour, sugars, baking powder, and salt. Add the unsweetened chocolate, eggs, oil, juice, rum, orange peel, and vanilla. Stir to combine. Add the chocolate chips and the almonds. Mix until the dough is well blended.

Preheat the oven to 350°. Shape the dough into a ball. Then divide the ball into 4 equal portions, shaping each section into a log about 2 inches wide by 12 to 14 inches long. Place 2 logs on each of 2 lightly greased baking sheets, and flatten the logs gently. Bake for 20 minutes. Remove from the oven and cool for 1 minute. Then cut diagonally into 1/2-inch-wide slices. Place the slices, cut-side down, on the baking sheets and return them to the oven to bake for an additional 15 minutes or until crisp. Cool on wire racks.

Meanwhile, melt the white chocolate in a double boiler over medium heat, stirring until smooth. (Vegetable oil may be added to the chocolate 1 teaspoon at a time if the chocolate is too thick for dipping.) Dip the tip of each cookie about 1 inch into the melted chocolate to coat. Lay on a wire rack until cool. Store in an airtight container.

—GINGERBREAD MANSION INN

Chocolate Carrot Bread

The mini-chocolate chips add just the right sweet counterpoint to the carrots. Pinehill serves this bread for breakfast or teatime.

Filling			2	teaspoons baking soda
8	ounces cream cheese, softened		2	teaspoons cinnamon
1/4	cup sugar		1	teaspoon salt
1	egg		1	cup coarsely chopped walnuts
1/4	cup mini-chocolate chips		1	pound carrots, grated
Batter			3	eggs
2	cups all-purpose flour		1	cup vegetable or canola oil
1 1/2	cups sugar		1	teaspoon vanilla extract
1/4	cup loosely packed brown sugar			

MAKES 1 LOAF

Preheat the oven to 350°. In a medium bowl, cream together the cheese, sugar, and egg. Fold in the chocolate chips and set aside.

In a large bowl, mix together the flour, sugars, baking soda, cinnamon, and salt.

Stir in the walnuts and grated carrots. In another medium bowl, beat the eggs. Add the oil, and stir in the vanilla. Blend until incorporated. Add to the dry ingredients, stirring just until moistened.

Grease a 9x5-inch loaf pan and pour three-fourths of the batter into the pan. Spread the cream cheese/chocolate mixture on top of the batter. Top with remaining batter. Bake in the oven for 1 hour or until a tester comes clean.

—PINEHILL B&B

Fudge Pie

This down-home recipe actually creates a gourmet treat. Serve warm with a scoop of chocolate chip mint or vanilla ice cream.

1/2	cup (1 stick) butter
3	1-ounce squares unsweetened chocolate
1	cup sugar
1/3	cup light corn syrup
1/4	cup all-purpose flour
1	teaspoon vanilla extract
1/4	teaspoon salt
3	eggs, slightly beaten
1	9-inch unbaked pie crust

MAKES 8 TO 10 SERVINGS

Preheat the oven to 350°. In a 2-quart saucepan, melt the butter and chocolate over very low heat, stirring constantly. Remove from the heat and stir in the sugar, corn syrup, flour, vanilla, and salt. Continue stirring until the mixture is well blended. Add the eggs and mix well. Pour the filling into the unbaked pie shell. Set the pie on a cookie sheet and bake for 30 to 35 minutes or until the filling is puffed and the center is firm.

—TRAIL'S END

Chocolate has most likely deteriorated if a grayish film has risen to the surface and the wrapper has become oily. This change happens when chocolate becomes warm and the fat rises to the surface, discoloring the chocolate. Store chocolate in a cool, dry place at about 60°.

Peanut Butter Pie with Chocolate Glaze

༄

Garnish this pie with a little bit of whipped cream and chocolate curls, for added character. The pie needs a few hours in the refrigerator, so begin early before serving time. This pie is so good that it almost brings tears to your eyes.

Crust

1	cup chocolate wafer crumbs
1/2	cup finely chopped pecans
1/3	cup (3/4 stick) unsalted butter, melted
2	tablespoons sugar
1/4	teaspoon cinnamon

Filling

1 1/4	cups creamy peanut butter
1	8-ounce package cream cheese, softened
1	cup powdered sugar
1 1/4	cups heavy cream
1	tablespoon vanilla extract

Glaze

1/2	cup half-and-half
4	ounces semisweet chocolate, coarsely chopped

MAKES 8 SERVINGS

In a medium bowl, mix together all of the ingredients for the pie crust. Press the crust firmly on the bottom and up the sides of a 10-inch pie pan. Place the crust into the freezer and prepare the filling.

In a large bowl of electric mixer, beat the peanut butter, cream cheese, and 1/2 cup of the sugar until smooth. In a smaller bowl, using clean beaters, beat the heavy cream with the remaining 1/2 cup of sugar and the vanilla until stiff peaks form. Stir half of this mixture into the peanut-butter mixture, folding well, then fold in the remaining cream mixture. (The filling will be thick.) Spread into the chilled pie crust and refrigerate until firm.

Prepare the glaze when ready to serve. In a small saucepan, bring the half-and-half to a boil. Reduce the heat and stir in the chocolate until smooth and melted. Cool slightly and pour overtop the pie, tilting for even distribution. Return the pie to the refrigerator for at least 1 hour. Garnish and serve.

—ASA RANSOM HOUSE

Black Forest Cobbler

~∞~

On an inn-to-inn chocolate trail in northern Illinois, this dessert is one of the most popular ones. Chocolate chips, cherry preserves, and a smooth custard melt in your mouth and lift your midday spirits.

Pastry Crust

2 1/2	cups all-purpose flour
3/4	cup sugar
3/4	cup (1 1/2 sticks) cold butter

Filling

1/2	teaspoon baking powder
1/2	teaspoon baking soda
3/4	cup sour cream
1	egg
1	teaspoon vanilla extract

Custard

8	ounces cream cheese, softened
1/4	cup sugar
1	egg

Topping

1/2	cup cherry preserves
1/3	cup semisweet chocolate chips

MAKES 8 TO 10 SERVINGS

*P*reheat the oven to 350°. Prepare the pastry crust by combining the flour, sugar, and butter. Blend until the mixture forms coarse crumbs. Measure 1 cup of the crust mixture. Set aside for the topping. Press the remainder of the crumbs into the bottom of a greased 9-inch springform pan.

In a large bowl, combine the baking powder, baking soda, sour cream, egg, and vanilla for the first filling layer. Mix well, then pour into the pan.

Prepare the custard layer. Blend together the cream cheese, sugar, and egg. When thoroughly combined, pour over the filling mixture in the pan.

Prepare the topping. Combine the preserves, chocolate chips, and the reserved 1 cup of crust mixture. Mix well and sprinkle overtop the custard. Bake for 50 minutes or until crust is slightly browned.

—PINEHILL B&B

Marbled Chocolate Fruits

⌒⌒⌒

Place these in your guest room before your visitors arrive and they may serve as a welcome pick-me-up. These also make splendid chocolates at turndown time.

6	ounces bittersweet chocolate, coarsely chopped
6	ounces white chocolate, coarsely chopped
15	or more pieces dried or candied fruit, such as apricots, cherries, dates, pitted prunes, candied orange peel

MAKES 15 TO 18 SERVINGS

Melt each kind of chocolate in separate saucepans over low heat. Cool the chocolates, stirring constantly, until they reach about 95° on a candy thermometer. Pour the cooled white and dark chocolate into a bowl. Using a kitchen knife, marble the chocolates, together by gently pulling the mixtures back and forth. Dip fruit pieces into the marbled mixture—dipping straight down and then straight up—so that the marbled pattern is reproduced on the fruit. Allow the chocolates to cool and harden on waxed paper.

—SEVEN SISTERS INN

Orange-Walnut Chocolate Tart

∽∾∽

An orange-spiced afternoon tea perfectly complements this pleasing dessert. The inn is situated against one of the most picturesque parks in the Midwest. Pack a picnic lunch and visit the falls—delightful.

LEFT AND ABOVE: THE TART IN A GUEST CABIN AT THE INN AT CEDAR FALLS, LOGAN, OHIO

Orange-Walnut Chocolate Tart (continued)

Crust		Filling	
1¼	cups all-purpose flour	1	cup orange marmalade
¼	cup powdered sugar	½	cup coarsely chopped walnuts
1	teaspoon salt	**Topping**	
⅓	cup (¾ stick) chilled butter	1	cup heavy cream
1	tablespoon cold water	2	cups chocolate chips

MAKES 8 TO 10 SERVINGS

Preheat the oven to 350°. Prepare the crust. In a food processor, combine the flour, sugar, and salt. Pulse until blended. Add the butter and process until the mixture forms coarse crumbs. Add the water and pulse until the dough pulls from the sides of the bowl. Press the dough against the bottom and sides of a lightly greased 10-inch tart pan. Bake for 10 to 12 minutes or until golden brown.

Meanwhile, make the filling. In a small bowl, combine the marmalade and nuts, mixing well. Pour into the prepared pie crust and set aside. Prepare the topping.

Bring the cream to a boil (over medium high heat) in a 1-quart saucepan. Remove the pan from the heat and stir in the chocolate chips. Continue stirring until the chips have melted and the mixture is smooth. Pour the melted chocolate over the pie filling, spreading evenly to the edges. Chill for at least 4 hours. Serve cold.

—THE INN AT CEDAR FALLS

RIGHT: LIKE THE INN AT CEDAR FALLS, THE MYSTICAL ASH CAVE IS A MAJOR ATTRACTION IN THE HOCKING HILLS OF SOUTHEASTERN OHIO.

Mocha Squares with Coffee Sauce

The recipe calls for instant-coffee granules. Experiment with a flavored coffee to make the squares even more interesting. Our testers loved this recipe and especially the coffee sauce, which they say you can also beat stiffly, turning it into a coffee cream for use in other recipes as well. Garnish with chocolate coffee beans. Seven Sisters Inn often appears in my cookbooks. The food from breakfast to teatime is creative and delicious.

5	ounces semisweet chocolate, coarsely chopped
3	tablespoons water
1	teaspoon instant coffee granules
1/2	cup (1 stick) unsalted butter, cut into pieces, at room temperature
4	eggs, separated
1/2	cup plus 2 tablespoons sugar
1/4	teaspoon cream of tartar
5	tablespoons all-purpose flour

Coffee Sauce

3/4	cup heavy cream
2	tablespoons sugar
2	teaspoons instant coffee granules

MAKES 8 TO 10 SERVINGS

*P*reheat the oven to 325°. Lightly grease an 8-inch square baking pan and line the bottom with waxed paper. Lightly grease and flour the paper. Melt the chocolate in a double boiler over simmering water. Stir in the water and the coffee. When smooth, blend in the butter. Remove the pan from the heat and allow the mixture to cool.

Beat the egg yolks in a large mixing bowl. Add the 1/2 cup of sugar and beat at high speed until the mixture is pale and very thick—about 4 to 5 minutes. In a separate bowl, beat the egg whites and the cream of tartar until stiff peaks form. Gradually add the remaining 2 tablespoons of sugar, beating at high speed until the whites are shiny and stiff.

With a large spoon, gently stir the chocolate mixture into the egg-yolk mixture. Sift the flour over the bowl and gently fold it in with a spatula. Fold in the egg whites next. Carefully transfer the batter into the prepared pan. Bake for about 40 minutes or until a tester comes clean. Cool on a wire rack. Cut the cake into equal squares.

Prepare the coffee sauce. In a large, chilled bowl, combine the cream, sugar, and coffee. Whip at medium speed until slightly thickened (do not form soft peaks). Serve with warm mocha squares.

—SEVEN SISTERS INN

Old-Fashioned Fudge Cake with Walnuts

∽•∾

Brownie-like but considerably lighter in texture, this simple cake is always a crowd pleaser. Serve warm with a favorite chocolate sauce and ice cream. Freeze leftover cake.

1¹/₄	cups (2 ¹/₂ sticks) butter
5	1-ounce squares semisweet chocolate, chopped
6	eggs
3	cups all-purpose flour
2¹/₂	cups sugar
1	cup coarsely chopped walnuts

MAKES UP TO 20 SERVINGS

In a small saucepan, melt the butter and chocolate over low heat, stirring frequently. Remove the pan from the heat and allow the chocolate to cool for about 30 minutes.

Preheat the oven to 350°. Whisk the eggs in a large mixing bowl. Set aside. In a separate bowl, combine the flour and sugar. Gently fold the dry ingredients into the eggs, stirring just until moist. Stir in the melted chocolate mixture.

Pour the batter into a 10x15-inch baking pan. Sprinkle with chopped walnuts. Bake for 25 minutes or until the top springs back when touched. Cut into squares of desired size.

—GAIL'S KITCHEN

Cream-Filled Chocolate and
Raspberry Cupcakes

‿o‿

My friends know that if there is one way to perk up my afternoon it is to get me a few of those old-fashioned Hostess cream-filled cupcakes. I devised these cakes to satisfy my nostalgic yearnings at home (and of course, they are far better than the packaged variety). These are fun to make and serve. When I really want to get down and decadent, I add a chocolate icing before adding the cream and raspberries to the top of the cupcake.

LEFT: CUPCAKE FOR THE PILLOW

A PARTY-TIME VERSION OF THE CHOCOLATE AND RASPBERRY CUPCAKES

In France, children spread chocolate on their bread as we spread jam or butter. See our recipe for Pain au Chocolat on page 8.

Cream–Filled Chocolate and Raspberry Cupcakes (continued)

Cupcakes

1/2	cup (1 stick) butter
1 1/2	cups sugar
2	cups sifted all-purpose flour
1	teaspoon baking soda
1/2	teaspoon salt
1	cup milk
3	eggs, beaten
2	1-ounce squares unsweetened chocolate

1	teaspoon vanilla extract
1	teaspoon lemon flavoring

Filling

1	pint fresh raspberries
2	tablespoons sugar
2	cups heavy cream, whipped
	Chocolate ganache or frosting, optional

MAKES 1 1/2 DOZEN CUPCAKES

*P*reheat the oven to 350°. Cream the butter and sugar in a large mixing bowl. In a separate bowl, sift the flour with the baking soda and salt. Slowly add the dry ingredients to the creamed mixture, alternating with 1/2 cup of the milk. Stir in the beaten eggs.

In a medium saucepan, combine the chocolate and the remaining 1/2 cup of milk. Stir over low heat until the chocolate melts. Cool slightly, then add to the batter. Mix well. Stir in the vanilla and lemon flavoring.

Pour the batter into greased 2 1/2-inch muffin tins, filling the cups about 2/3 full. Bake for 25 minutes or until a tester comes clean. Remove the cupcakes from the pan and cool on a wire rack.

Toss the raspberries with the sugar, coating evenly. Cut the tops off the cooled cupcakes. Set aside. Carefully scoop out a little of the interior of each cake. Fill the cavity with sugared raspberries and a little whipped cream. Add the cake top and ice, if desired, at this point or just garnish with whipped cream and a few raspberries.

—GAIL'S KITCHEN

Raspberry Cream Puffs with Chocolate Ganache

⌒o⌒

Asa Ransom House has given us a recipe for puff pastry shells. If you are in a hurry, use the prepared packaged shells.

Pastry
1/2	cup water
1/8	teaspoon salt
1/4	cup (1/2 stick) butter
1/2	cup all-purpose flour
2	eggs at room temperature

Filling
1	16-ounce package frozen raspberries

2	tablespoons cornstarch
1/4	cup water
1	cup heavy cream
1	teaspoon powdered sugar
1/4	teaspoon vanilla extract

Ganache
4	ounces semisweet chocolate
1/2	cup heavy cream

Here is how to make an all-purpose chocolate cream cheese spread or topping. Cream together 2 tablespoons butter and 4 ounces cream cheese. To that mixture, add 1 1/2 ounces unsweetened chocolate (melted), 1/8 teaspoon salt, 1 1/2 cups sifted powdered sugar, 1/4 cup heavy cream, and 1/2 teaspoon vanilla extract. Mix well and serve.

Preheat the oven to 400°. Prepare the cream puff. In a medium saucepan, combine the water, salt, and butter. Bring to a boil. Add the flour and stir until the dough forms a ball. Transfer the dough to a bowl and beat in the eggs—one at a time— mixing until thoroughly blended. Scoop the dough into a 16-inch pastry bag fitted with a large star-shaped tip. Squeeze the dough onto a cookie sheet in 3-inch circles, adding enough dough to make each circle 2 layers high. Use up all the dough to make about 4 cream puffs. Bake for 10 minutes. Reduce the heat to 350° and bake for 20 to 25 minutes or until firm and crisp to the touch.

Meanwhile, prepare the filling. Thaw and strain the raspberries, reserving the excess liquid. Place the raspberry liquid in a small saucepan and bring to a boil. Mix together the cornstarch and water. Slowly add to the raspberry liquid, stirring constantly, until the sauce has thickened. Remove from the heat and cool completely. Fold in the raspberries.

Cut the cream puffs in half horizontally. Spoon the raspberry mixture into each puff. Set aside. Whip 1 cup heavy cream with the sugar and vanilla until stiff peaks form. Scoop the whipped cream over the raspberry filling. Top with the remaining cream puff halves.

Prepare the ganache. Combine the chocolate and heavy cream in a saucepan over low heat, stirring until the chocolate just melts. Pour over the filled cream puffs and refrigerate until the chocolate hardens. Serve cold.

—ASA RANSOM HOUSE

Evening Expressions

Peppermint Parfaits with Chocolate Sauce

∽∾∾

This recipe makes a mousse that is a Durham House specialty. The Victorian mansion is well appointed with lace and gentle reminders of another time, as is this light and refreshing ending to a meal. The recipe calls for those red-and-white, hard peppermint candies in cellophane wrappers.

1/2	pound hard peppermint candies		3	drops red food coloring
1/2	cup half-and-half		1 1/2	cups heavy cream
1	small envelope unflavored gelatin			Chocolate sauce
1	tablespoon cold water			Mint sprigs for garnish

MAKES 8 SERVINGS

Finely chop the peppermint candy in a food processor. Transfer the chopped candy to a double boiler set over simmering water. Add the half-and-half and stir constantly until the candy dissolves.

Dissolve the gelatin in cold water. Stir into the peppermint mixture, making sure all of the gelatin is dissolved. Remove from the heat and allow the mixture to cool.

Meanwhile, add the red food coloring to the cream in another bowl, and whip until stiff. Fold into the cooled peppermint mixture. Serve peppermint mousse in individual dessert dishes such as parfait glasses. Drizzle with homemade or bottled chocolate sauce and garnish with sprigs of fresh mint.

—DURHAM HOUSE

Iced Chocolate Cappuccino

꙳

Gingerbread Mansion receives a lot of attention and rightfully so. Tucked into the enchanting little village of Ferndale, California, it is an inn where dreams do come true. Chef Larry Martin gets you on the right road with a cappuccino that does not require a machine to make.

1	pint coffee ice cream	1/2	cup half-and-half
1	ounce cognac	1/4	teaspoon cinnamon
1	ounce crème de cocoa (cacao)		Whipped cream and shaved chocolate for garnish
2	tablespoons chocolate syrup		

MAKES 2 SERVINGS

Combine all ingredients in a blender. Mix until smooth and creamy. Pour the mixture into stemmed glasses. Garnish with whipped cream and shaved chocolate.

—GINGERBREAD MANSION

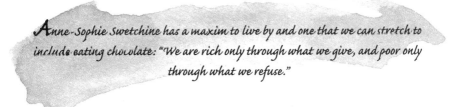

Anne-Sophie Swetchine has a maxim to live by and one that we can stretch to include eating chocolate: "We are rich only through what we give, and poor only through what we refuse."

Raspberry-Almond Pâté

∽◦∾

I like this recipe for company because you can leave it out on the dessert table and guests can help themselves. The pâté is delicious served by the slice with raspberries and almonds or spread onto light sweet biscuits. This pâté needs a chilling time, so prepare in advance. Raspberry chips are just becoming available. Our testers added raspberry flavoring to vanilla chips.

1	cup finely-ground toasted almonds		1	cup semisweet mini-chocolate chips
1¼	cups heavy cream		1	teaspoon almond extract
¼	cup (½ stick) butter			Fresh raspberries and sliced almonds for garnish
12	ounces raspberry or chocolate chips			

MAKES UP TO 20 SERVINGS

Line a 9x5-inch loaf pan with waxed paper. Sprinkle the ground almonds on the bottom.

In a medium saucepan, simmer the cream and butter over medium heat. Reduce the temperature to low and add the raspberry and chocolate chips. Stir until the chips

have melted and the mixture is smooth. Remove from the heat. Stir in the almond extract and pour the mixture into the prepared pan. Place in the refrigerator and chill for at least 5 hours or until set.

Invert the pan onto a serving platter to unmold. Remove the waxed paper and cut the pâté into ½-inch slices.

—PINEHILL B&B

[65]

Peanut Butter and Chocolate Strawberry Fondue

Whatever the time of year, I can always count on this recipe to get rave reviews. It is easy to prepare, and fondue, as always, heats up good conversation and entertainment. Most often, I use large strawberries because they are plump and easier to dip. Get enough to make an impressive dish. Use leftovers for another recipe or for breakfast. You may also use orange sections, bananas, pound cake, or any other bite-size food you desire. Give everyone a fondue fork and a small plate, and dip in.

4	1-ounce squares unsweetened chocolate
1	cup light cream
1	cup sugar
$1/4$	cup smooth peanut butter
$1^1/_2$	teaspoons vanilla extract
$1^1/_2$	teaspoons almond extract

MAKES 4 SERVINGS

*H*eat the chocolate and cream in a medium saucepan over medium low heat. Stir constantly until the chocolate has melted. When the mixture is smooth and well blended, add the sugar and the peanut butter. Stirring constantly, continue cooking until the mixture thickens slightly. Remove from the heat. Stir in the vanilla and transfer the mixture to a fondue pot.

— GAIL'S KITCHEN

LEFT: PINEHILL B&B ADDS MANY FLAVORS TO ITS FUDGE—FROM MINT TO GRAND MARNIER OR EVEN PEANUT BUTTER, OF COURSE.

Crème de Mocha Custard Pots

꧁꧂

Custard is one dessert that never fails to please. The puddinglike consistency of this traditional meal-ender offers a note of nostalgia for the memory books. I like the mocha touch provided by the equally memorable Seven Sisters Inn.

An easy chocolate for the pillow is this recipe from Highland Farm. Cream together 1/2 cup margarine with powdered sugar, 1 1/2 cups peanut butter, and 1 teaspoon vanilla extract. Dip the mixture in melted mixture of 1/4 block paraffin and 6 ounces mini-chocolate chips.

4	ounces semisweet chocolate
1½	cups milk
2	tablespoons instant coffee granules
4	egg yolks
5	tablespoons sugar

MAKES 4 SERVINGS

*P*reheat the oven to 350°. Combine the chocolate and ½ cup of the milk in a medium saucepan. Stir over low heat until the chocolate has just about melted. Remove the chocolate from the stove and whisk until the mixture is smooth. In a small saucepan, bring the remaining cup of milk to a boil. Remove from the heat and whisk in the coffee. Cool for about 3 minutes, then gradually whisk the milk into the chocolate mixture.

In a large bowl, lightly whisk the egg yolks until just broken up. Add the sugar and whisk until blended. Gradually add ¾ cup of the chocolate mixture in a thin stream, stirring constantly. Using a wooden spoon, gradually stir in the remaining chocolate mixture. Strain into a large measuring cup. Skim the foam that develops on the surface.

Arrange 4 (3 ½-inch) ramekins or custard cups in a shallow baking dish. Divide the custard mixture evenly among the ramekins. Fill the baking dish halfway up the sides of the ramekins with hot, but not boiling, water. Cover loosely with a sheet of foil (do not seal the edges). Bake for about 25 minutes or until the top is set and jiggles slightly when the pan is moved. Remove the custard cups from the water bath and cool on a wire rack. Cover and refrigerate 3 hours before serving. This custard can only keep 1 day in the refrigerator, so serve immediately.

—SEVEN SISTERS INN

*W*hite Chocolate Fettuccine with Strawberry Sauce

꼭⊙◌

If you really want to impress your guests, this dessert will have them talking for weeks to come. Imagine making a pasta shape with white chocolate and serving it with fruit and a fruit sauce.

Fettuccine

7	ounces white chocolate, melted
1/4	cup light corn syrup
1	cup powdered sugar

Strawberries

24	large ripe strawberries, washed and patted dry

1/2	cup or more Amaretto liqueur
8	ounces semisweet chocolate, melted

Sauce

24	medium-size ripe strawberries

MAKES 8 SERVINGS

*I*n a small bowl, mix together the white chocolate and corn syrup until a soft dough forms. Gently roll out the chocolate on waxed paper to a thickness of 1/8-inch. Refrigerate until hardened.

Run the chocolate through a pasta machine to cut (fettuccine style), or using a sharp knife, cut the chocolate into thin strips, about 1/3-inch wide. While cutting, let the strips fall into a pile of the powdered sugar to prevent sticking. Refrigerate until ready to serve.

Using a cooking syringe, inject 24 of the strawberries with a squirt of Amaretto. Then dip each berry into the melted dark chocolate. Place the strawberries on waxed paper and refrigerate until the chocolate hardens.

Prepare the sauce. Purée the remaining 24 strawberries in a blender until smooth. Pour the purée through a fine mesh strainer. Pour the sauce onto individual serving plates. Add a few fettuccine noodles and top with 3 chocolate-covered strawberries per plate.

—THE CHECKERBERRY INN

Chocolate-Truffle Cheesecake with Raspberry Sauce

You will need to begin preparing this cake a day ahead of serving time. This cheesecake is gentle on the egg count. Rowell's is the epitome of a country inn—small, historic, beautifully appointed, on-hand innkeepers, and fabulous food served in a small dining room.

Crust			1	cup sugar
2¹/₂	cups chocolate wafer crumbs		2	eggs
¹/₃	cup (³/₄ stick) butter, melted		2	tablespoons heavy cream
¹/₂	cup sugar		1	teaspoon vanilla extract
Filling			¹/₄	cup Chambord liqueur
1	8-ounce package semisweet chocolate, cut into ¹/₂-inch cubes		*Sauce*	
			1	10-ounce package frozen raspberries, thawed, juice reserved
¹/₄	cup strong, brewed hot coffee			
3	8-ounce packages cream cheese		2	teaspoons cornstarch
1	cup sour cream			

MAKES 8 TO 10 SERVINGS

P*reheat the oven to 375°. Prepare the crust. Blend together the chocolate crumbs, butter, and the ¹/₂ cup of sugar. Press the mixture into the bottom and part way up the sides of a 9-inch springform pan. Set aside.*

Finely grind the chocolate cubes in a food processor. With the food processor running, pour in the hot coffee. Process until the chocolate is melted. Add the cream cheese, sour cream, sugar, eggs, heavy cream, vanilla, and the liqueur. Process until smooth, a few minutes. Stop to scrape the sides when necessary.

Pour the mixture into the prepared pan and bake for 55 minutes. The center should still be soft. Let cool at room temperature. Cover and chill at least 8 hours.

Prepare the raspberry sauce. In a small saucepan, combine the raspberry juice with the cornstarch, stirring over medium heat until smooth and thickened. Remove from the heat and cool. To serve, place a pool of the sauce in the center of an individual serving plate, add a slice of the cake, and serve.

—ROWELL'S INN

[73]

Cocoa Kahlua Cake with Chocolate Glaze

∽o∾

Vanilla yogurt moistens this cake that has a hint of java and the soft crunch of chocolate chips. Strain the yogurt through a fine mesh sieve for 2 to 3 hours before adding it to the cake batter.

The cake should be made a day ahead of serving time so that the glaze sets well. This royal cake is as elegant as the inn itself and as warm as the innkeepers.

When melting chocolate, do so over hot (not boiling) water as chocolate scorches easily and the steam from the boiling water may harden or stiffen the chocolate.

Cake

1	cup granulated sugar
1/2	cup quality unsweetened cocoa, plus more for pan preparation
1	cup vanilla yogurt, strained
1/4	cup Kahlua
1/2	cup (1 stick) butter, softened
1	cup superfine sugar
2	eggs
2	cups cake flour
1	teaspoon baking soda
1/2	teaspoon salt

6	ounces chocolate chips

Glaze

9	ounces semisweet chocolate, coarsely chopped
2	ounces unsweetened chocolate
1 1/2	tablespoons unsalted butter
3/4	cup heavy cream
1	tablespoon Kahlua
	Chocolate icing for garnish
	Whole pecans for garnish

MAKES 20 SERVINGS

*P*reheat the oven to 350°. Grease a 10-inch tube pan and dust with cocoa powder.

In a small bowl, blend together the granulated sugar, cocoa, and 1/2 cup of the yogurt. In another small bowl mix the remaining yogurt with the Kahlua, setting it aside. In a medium bowl, cream together the butter and the superfine sugar. Add the eggs, one at a time, beating well after each addition. Add the flour, 1 cup at a time. Then slowly beat in the cocoa mixture, alternating with the remaining yogurt/Kahlua mixture. Fold in the chocolate chips. Pour into the prepared pan and bake for about 1 hour or until a tester comes clean. Cool on a cake rack before removing from the pan.

Prepare the glaze. Melt the chocolates over a double boiler. Add the butter, cream, and Kahlua. Cover tightly and heat over medium high heat for a few minutes (do not boil). Remove the cover and stir gently for a few minutes more or until the mixture is completely melted and smooth. Transfer to a stainless steel bowl, cover, and let stand at room temperature until it cools down to warm.

Remove the cake from the pan and transfer to a flat cake dish. Slowly pour about half of the glaze over the top of the cake, spreading it evenly on top and down the sides with a metal spatula. Refrigerate the cake until the glaze is firm, a couple of hours or so. Repeat with the remaining glaze, returning the cake to the refrigerator. Serve when the glaze has firmed up again. Decorate with your favorite chocolate icing and whole pecans, if desired.

—SAMPSON EAGON INN

*F*lourless Chocolate Cake with Fruit Purée

വ്ഗ

This flourless recipe makes a dense, rich cake. Serve thin slices and do not fret over the nine eggs. Remember there are plenty of servings here. It is very important to cook the cake slowly. Make a fruit purée garnish by adding fresh fruit to a blender with sugar to taste. Blend until smooth.

1	cup (2 sticks) butter		9	eggs, at room temperature
1	pound bittersweet chocolate		1/2	tablespoon vanilla extract
1 1/2	cups sugar			Powdered sugar for garnish
1/8	teaspoon salt			Fruit purée and fresh fruit of choice, for garnish
1/2	cup hazelnut liqueur			

MAKES 12 TO 14 SERVINGS

*P*reheat the oven to 325°. In a large saucepan, combine the butter and chocolate. Melt slowly over low heat. In a large mixing bowl, combine the sugar, salt, hazelnut liqueur, eggs, and vanilla. Beat at high speed until the mixture has almost tripled in volume—about 10 to 15 minutes. Carefully fold the egg mixture into the chocolate. Pour the batter into a greased 9-inch springform pan. Bake for about 1 hour or until a tester comes clean. The cake will rise higher than the top of the pan. When cool, a crispy crust will form on the cake and cave in. Garnish with the fruit purées and white chocolate leaves, if desired.

—THE FAIRMOUNT

Mocha Bourbon Pound Cake with Cream Cheese Icing and Fresh Blackberries

Sometimes the simplest desserts can be the most complementary to a meal. This gourmet version of a pound cake is enhanced by updated flavorful ingredients. If blackberries are not in season, serve the cake with raspberries.

Cake

1½	cups freshly brewed espresso coffee
½	cup bourbon
1½	cups sugar
6	ounces semisweet chocolate
1	cup unsalted butter
1	tablespoon vanilla extract
2	eggs
2	cups all-purpose flour
1	tablespoon baking soda
½	teaspoon salt

Icing

8	ounces cream cheese, softened
2	tablespoons orange juice
2½	cups powdered sugar
	Fresh blackberries, lightly tossed with sugar

MAKES 8 TO 10 SERVINGS

*P*reheat the oven to 325°. In a large bowl, stir together the coffee, bourbon, and sugar; set aside.

Combine the chocolate and the butter in a double boiler. Stir until the chocolate melts. When smooth, whisk in the coffee mixture. In a mixing bowl, lightly beat the vanilla and the eggs. Stir in a little of the warm chocolate/coffee mixture. When combined, mix the entire egg mixture into the chocolate/coffee batter.

Sift together the flour, baking soda, and salt. Gradually stir the flour mixture into the batter, mixing until very smooth. Pour the batter into a greased and floured 10-inch loaf pan. Bake for 45 minutes to 1 hour or until a tester comes clean. Cool for 10 minutes before removing from the pan. Cool completely before icing.

Cream together the softened cream cheese and orange juice. Gradually whip in the sugar until the icing is smooth and fluffy. Spread over the cooled mocha bourbon pound cake. Serve with fresh blackberries.

—FLYING M RANCH

Suite
Dreams

———

∾⫘∾

Mini-Devil Cheesecakes

∞

Just the right amount of sweet and savory before bedtime, this easy recipe can be made ahead and frozen, so that you can take out the cheesecakes as needed. This dish is also a good buffet recipe or an item for a covered dish supper. Devilishly good, these heavenly cakes will make your guests think you are an angel of the sea, too, once they take a bite.

PICTURE FACING CHAPTER OPENER: GINGERBREAD MANSION, FERNDALE, CALIFORNIA

1⅓	cups graham cracker crumbs	3	8-ounce packages cream cheese, softened
⅓	cup sugar		
¼	cup unsweetened cocoa	14	ounces sweetened condensed milk
⅓	cup (¾ stick) butter, melted		
2	12-ounce packages semisweet chocolate chips	3	eggs
		2½	teaspoons vanilla extract

MAKES 30 CAKES

*P*reheat the oven to 300°. In a large bowl, stir together the graham cracker crumbs, sugar, cocoa, and butter. Press equal portions into paper-lined mini-muffin tins.

In a small saucepan, melt 1 package of the chocolate chips over low heat. Meanwhile, beat the cheese in the large bowl of an electric mixer until fluffy. Gradually add the condensed milk and the melted chocolate, beating until smooth. Add the eggs and vanilla, mixing well.

Spoon the batter into the prepared tins. Top the mini cheesecakes with the remaining chocolate chips. Bake for 20 minutes or until set. Cool completely, then refrigerate before serving.

—ANGEL OF THE SEA

*I*nnkeepers suggest that you bring chocolates for the pillow to your guest's room close to bedtime if you are afraid the chocolates will melt. If you must leave chocolate out all day, they suggest making chocolates with candy coating or paraffin.

Chocolate Raspberry Cordials

✺

Nothing says "Good night, we are glad you are here" more than chocolate-covered cordials. Use only fresh berries. Our testers found that frozen raspberries were too messy for chocolates on the pillow. They also found that fresh pitted cherries work well.

1/4	cup heavy cream		12	ounces semisweet chocolate chips
1/4	cup Chambord liqueur		2 to 3	dozen fresh raspberries

MAKES UP TO 3 DOZEN

Combine the heavy cream and Chambord in a saucepan. Bring to a boil over medium high heat. Reduce the heat to low and add the chocolate chips, stirring just until they are completely melted. Remove from the heat.

Carefully spoon the chocolate mixture into tiny fluted candy paper cups until about two-thirds full. (Do this in a mini-muffin baking tin to hold the papers in place as you fill them.) Push a fresh or frozen raspberry into the middle of each until it is about halfway submerged. Chill until firm. These cordials may be kept in the freezer and defrosted just before serving.

—SEA CREST BY THE SEA

Always use a quality chocolate when preparing a recipe. Fresh chocolate is shiny brown and free of lumps, tiny bubbles, and white specks.

Chocolate Mudslide Drink

∾০৲∾

Named by the innkeepers because New England can be a sea of mud during the spring thaw, this pleasant beverage is a perfect close to the day in any season. Innkeepers Laura and Jayme Simoes have decorated the inn with a 1940s atmosphere. Antique radios in each guest room will dial up old radio shows Jayme pipes up in the evenings.

THE TEA ROOM OF THE INN AT MAPLEWOOD FARM, HILLSBOROUGH, NEW HAMPSHIRE

*W*hen recipes call for cocoa powder, do not use cocoa mixes that have added
ingredients such as sugar and flavorings.

Chocolate Mudslide Drink (continued)

3	cups ice cubes
1	ounce vodka
1	ounce Kahlua
1	ounce Bailey's Irish Cream
2	scoops chocolate ice cream

MAKES 2 SERVINGS

Place all ingredients in a blender and blend until smooth. Serve in a tall, thin glass.

—INN AT MAPLEWOOD FARM

Kissed by a Bonbon

∽ᴑᴍ

What could be more romantic than ending the day with a kiss—a chocolate one. The chocolate kiss is submerged in a cookie dough, a surprise inside a tiny, round bundle. The cookies freeze well.

3/4	cup vegetable shortening		1 1/4	cups all-purpose flour
1/2	cup sugar		1/2	teaspoon baking powder
1/4	cup brown sugar, firmly packed		1/2	teaspoon salt
1	egg		1/2	cup finely chopped pecans
2	teaspoons vanilla extract		36	chocolate kisses, unwrapped
1/2	teaspoon almond extract			Sifted powdered sugar

MAKES 3 DOZEN

Combine the shortening and sugars in a large mixing bowl. Beat with an electric mixer until light and fluffy. Add the egg and the extracts, mixing well. In a separate bowl, combine the flour, baking powder, salt, and pecans. Add to the creamed mixture, stirring until well blended.

Preheat the oven to 350°. Shape the batter into 36 1-inch balls. Press each ball around a chocolate kiss, covering completely. Arrange the bonbons on ungreased cookie sheets. Bake for 12 to 14 minutes, or until just starting to turn a light golden color. Cool slightly on wire racks. Roll the cookies in powdered sugar while still slightly warm, then cool completely before serving.

—GAIL'S KITCHEN

LEFT: FUDGE FOR SALE AT PINEHILL B&B

Chocolate-Dipped Maplenut Creams

✁∞✁

You will always find chocolates on the pillow at the elegant Gingerbread Mansion. The innkeepers say good night here in many other ways, too—there's bubble bath, a little liqueur, and, sometimes, a night massage.

1	cup heavy cream		1/2	cup marshmallow creme
1/2	cup milk		1	tablespoon maple extract
1/3	cup light corn syrup		1	cup coarsely chopped walnuts
4	cups sugar		1	pound chocolate, melted
1/4	teaspoon salt			

MAKES 52 SERVINGS

In a heavy 4 to 6-quart saucepan (nonstick preferred), combine the cream, milk, corn syrup, sugar, and salt. Stir over medium heat with a wooden spoon until the sugar dissolves and the mixture comes to a boil. Make sure the spoon does not touch the sides of the pan. If necessary, brush down the sides of the pan with a wet pastry brush to dissolve any sugar crystals that might remain.

Insert a candy thermometer and cook, stirring occasionally, until the mixture reaches a soft ball stage (240°). Remove the pan from the heat, and without stirring or scraping, pour the mixture into a 9x13-inch baking dish. Place in a cool area until barely lukewarm. Pour onto a marble slab, and with a wide-blade, clean paint scraper, or pastry trowel, work the fondant back and forth for about 10 to 15 minutes; then add the marshmallow creme, maple flavoring, and nuts on top. Continue working the batch until it becomes very stiff and loses its gloss, about 30 minutes. Form into 3/4-inch balls. Dip each ball in the melted chocolate and set the candies on a tray lined with waxed paper to harden.

—GINGERBREAD MANSION

LEFT: THE PALATIAL EMPIRE SUITE AT GINGERBREAD MANSION

Mints on the Pillow

❧

"And they leave mints on the pillow at turndown time" was a phrase often found in guidebooks when the B&B movement really caught on. Today mints for the pillow are only one of the amenities that range from whirlpool tubs to fireplaces in the rooms.

2¹/₂	pounds semisweet dark chocolate		1	teaspoon peppermint oil
1	pound margarine, melted and cooled slightly		1	teaspoon cognac
			2	pounds chocolate, melted

MAKES 96 CHOCOLATES

Melt the dark chocolate in a double boiler. Use a candy thermometer to test the temperature. Do not exceed 120°. Whisk the melted dark chocolate into the margarine. Mix well. Cool at room temperature to a soft stage, about 30 minutes. Add the peppermint oil and liqueur. Whip until light and fluffy. Pour the mixture onto an 8x12-inch waxed paper-lined tray and refrigerate until set. Cut into 1-inch squares. Dip each square into the melted milk chocolate and return the candies to the paper-lined tray. Refrigerate until the chocolate hardens.

—GINGERBREAD MANSION

You can eat chocolate without guilt if you believe what Miss Piggy has to say:
"Never eat more than you can lift."

GINGERBREAD MANSION, ONE OF THE MOST PHOTOGRAPHED INNS IN AMERICA

Add chocolate chips to pancake batter and you have chocolate pancakes.

Kahlua Chocolate Truffles

෴

1/3	cup heavy cream
1	tablespoon butter
6	ounces semisweet chocolate, chopped
1	teaspoon Kahlua
4	ounces milk chocolate
	Unsweetened cocoa for dusting

MAKES 12 TRUFFLES

Combine the cream and butter in a saucepan. Bring to a boil. Pour the cream-and-butter mixture over the chocolate in a large mixing bowl. Add the Kahlua and stir until smooth. Chill in the refrigerator for 1 to 2 hours or until set.

Using 2 teaspoons, shape the chilled chocolate mixture into 1-inch balls, rolling with the palms of your hands, and set aside on waxed paper. Chill for 1 hour. Melt the milk chocolate. Dip the chilled balls in the milk chocolate and immediately roll each in cocoa. Refrigerate for 2 to 3 hours or until the chocolate hardens. Store in an airtight container between layers of waxed paper.

—A CAMBRIDGE HOUSE

*U*se a vegetable peeler and long strokes to make chocolate curls.

Chocolate Bavarian

❀

This mousselike dessert makes a particularly attractive one for setting by the bedside or serving by the fire as the midnight embers burn. Innkeeper and Chef Yvonne Martin serves up hearty meals that are beautifully presented at the White Oak Inn. If you're watching cholesterol, you can omit the egg yolks.

¹/₄	cup sugar		1	cup semisweet chocolate chips
1	small envelope unflavored gelatin		3	egg yolks
¹/₄	teaspoon salt		1	cup heavy cream
1³/₄	cups milk		1	teaspoon vanilla extract

MAKES 6 TO 8 SERVINGS

In a heavy-bottomed saucepan, combine the sugar, gelatin, salt, milk, and chocolate chips. Place over medium heat and stir until the chocolate melts.

Beat the egg yolks just slightly. Whisk ¹/₄ cup of the melted chocolate mixture into the

egg yolks, then pour the yolk mixture into the saucepan with the remainder of the chocolate. Reduce the temperature to low and cook for 2 minutes, stirring constantly. Remove the saucepan from the heat and cover with plastic wrap. Place the covered pan in a sink filled with ice water. Chill, stirring occasionally, until partially set—about 20 to 30 minutes. Meanwhile, beat the heavy cream until stiff. Blend in the vanilla. Fold the whipped cream into the thickened chocolate mixture. Serve the Bavarian in champagne flutes or white wine glasses. Garnish with grated chocolate.

—WHITE OAK INN

Chocolate Jammin' Tassies

~⊶~

I have no doubt that Mark Twain or at least Huck Finn would have enjoyed coming home to these little treats after a day of fishing by water's edge. Guests at Garth Woodside Mansion come back to the inn after sightseeing in Hannibal, Missouri, Mark Twain country. These tassies are cookie-dough cups or shells filled with chocolate and jam. You need to start the recipe a few hours or a day ahead of serving time.

Bittersweet chocolate has more flavor than milk chocolate does.

Shells

1/2	cup (1 stick) butter, softened
1	3-ounce package cream cheese, softened
3	teaspoons sugar
1/2	teaspoon vanilla extract
1	cup sifted all-purpose flour
1/2	cup finely chopped walnuts

Filling

1/4	cup raspberry, strawberry, or apricot jam
2	1-ounce squares semisweet chocolate
1	tablespoon butter

MAKES 24

*P*reheat the oven to 350°. Prepare the dough for the tassie shells. In a medium bowl, beat the butter, cream cheese, sugar, and vanilla until light and fluffy. Stir in the flour. When smooth, add the nuts and blend well. Wrap the dough in plastic wrap and refrigerate for a few hours or overnight.

Grease 24 mini-muffin cups. To form the tassie shells, gently press the dough in the bottom and up the sides of the mini-cups. Bake for 12 minutes or until lightly browned. Remove from the oven and cool slightly on wire racks. Carefully loosen the shells with the tip of a paring knife and lift out of cups. Cool completely.

When tassie shells are cool, spoon about 1/2 teaspoon of jam into each, leaving about 1/8 inch of space at the top. Melt the chocolate and butter in a double boiler over hot, but not boiling, water. Cool slightly. Spoon a layer of the chocolate mixture over the jam layer. Refrigerate until the chocolate sets—about 1 hour. Chill until ready to serve.

—GARTH WOODSIDE MANSION

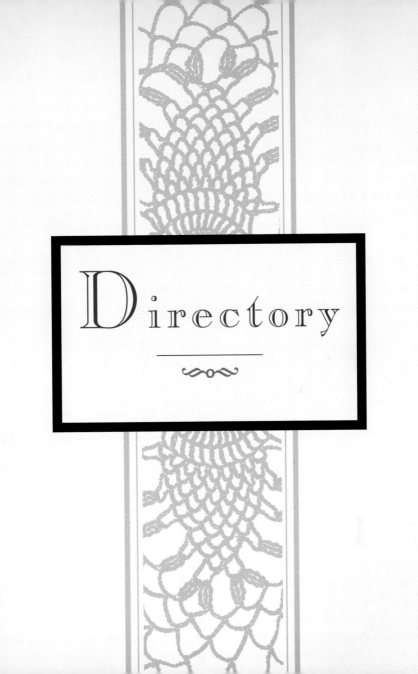

Directory

Angel of the Sea
5 Trenton Avenue
Cape May, NJ 08204
(609) 884-3369

Rooms: 27

Open year-round, this historic inn is indeed heaven-sent. Most of the rooms feature sunny ocean views and local Victorian antiques. Full breakfast, afternoon tea, and a wine-and-cheese hour are just a few of the inn's amenities.

Asa Ransom House
10529 Main Street
Clarence, NY 14031
(716) 759-2315

Rooms: 6 rooms, 3 suites

After shopping for antiques in Clarence, spend the night at the cozy Asa Ransom House. Enjoy country gourmet meals and fine New York State wines in a relaxing, historic environment.

Blue Harbor House
67 Elm Street
Camden, ME 04843
(203) 236-3196

Rooms: 10

Up the hill from one of America's most picturesque harbors, this inn is not only known for its breakfasts because its lobster dinners are the best anywhere.

A Cambridge House
2218 Massachusetts Avenue
Cambridge, MA 02140
(617) 491-6300

Rooms: 16

In the heart of everything Boston— from Harvard Square to the Freedom Trail, this sumptuous urban inn is deliciously appointed from the plate to the bed chambers.

The Checkerberry Inn
62644 CR 37
Goshen, IN 46526
(219) 642-4445

Rooms: 11 rooms, 3 suites

Miles of pastoral rolling farmland is what you see from your bedroom at the Checkerberry Inn. Situated on 100 acres in the heart of Indiana's Amish country, this comfortable inn is a sanctuary from the toils of everyday life.

Durham House
921 Heights Boulevard
Houston, TX 77008
(713) 868-4654

Rooms: 5

Marguerite Swanson is the kind of innkeeper you wish lived next door to you. From the way she dresses to the way she decorates and cooks, everything is romantic. The room named Heart's Desire is only one reason to stop here for the night.

The Fairmount Hotel
401 South Alamo Street
San Antonio, TX 78205
(210) 224-8800

Rooms: 37

You would not expect such elegance in the heart of San Antonio, a bustling city of the Old West, but it is here, and Chef Sander Edmondson's cuisine is truly some of the finest—if not the finest—in the city.

Flying M Ranch
23029 N.W. Flying M Road
Yamhill, OR 97148
(503) 662-3222

Rooms: 35

You'll see more planes than cars in the parking lot of this rustic Oregon log lodge. The cuisine here is so popular that people get here any way they can for the innkeeper's hearty home-style meals.

Garth Woodside Mansion
R.R. #1
Hannibal, MO 63401
(314) 221-2789

Rooms: 8

The flying staircase is only one of the magnificent architectural structures of this special house. The breakfast is served family-style with individual gourmet selections. Guests often request recipes.

The Gingerbread Mansion Inn
400 Berding Street
P.O. Box 40
Ferndale, CA 95540
(707) 786-4000

Rooms: 11

This enchanting mansion looks as if it came straight out of a fairy tale. Live happily ever after for a few days while enjoying a fireside bubble bath, bedside chocolates, and afternoon tea. It deserves all of the recognition it receives worldwide.

Highland Farm
4145 Tower Hill Road
Wakefield, RI 02879
(401) 783-2408

Rooms: 3

The inn's chocolate-peanut balls are usually found in the generous cookie can, and guests can help themselves to these delicious treats all day at this 1800s farmhouse on twenty-eight acres.

The Inn at Buckeystown
c/o General Delivery
3521 Buckeystown Pike
Buckeystown, MD 21717
(301) 874-5755

Rooms: 6

Civil War history abounds in the village of Buckeystown. The inn, housed in a 19th-century mansion and also in a former church, offers comfortable and elegant lodging overlooking the landmark town.

The Inn at Cedar Falls
21190 St. Rt. 374
Logan, OH 43138
(614) 385-7489

Rooms: 12

This rustic log cabin inn is surrounded by the natural beauty of the Appalachian foothills. Mountain-style folk furniture and rag rugs create a cozy and authentic environment for country-gourmet dining.

The Inn at Maplewood Farm
447 Center Road
Hillsborough, NH 03244
(603) 464-4242

Rooms: 5

When this inn was built in 1794, folks probably did not have the kind of service offered at this fine country home today.

Manor House Inn
612 Hughes Street
Cape May, NJ 08204
(609) 884-4710

Rooms: 9

A turn-of-the-century experience in the heart of historic Cape May awaits guests of this inn. From the comfortable porch, guests can smell the aroma of homemade sticky buns fresh out of the innkeeper's oven.

Pinehill B&B
400 Mix Street
Oregon, IL 61061
(815) 732-2061

Rooms: 6

Home of the Blackhawk Chocolate Trail, this 1874 Italianate mansion is graced with romance in its architecture, antiques, and service.

Rowell's Inn
R.R. #1, Box 267-D
Simonsville, VT 05143
(802) 875-3658

Rooms: 5

Once a stagecoach stop, post office, and general store, this inn is one of my all-time favorites. Sleep where the town's VIPs once danced the night away. Gourmet comfort food is served here with great love and care.

Sampson Eagon Inn
238 East Beverley Street
Staunton, VA 24401
(703) 886-8200

Rooms: 5

Luxury in an historic setting best describes this thoughtful inn of the Shenandoah Valley, featured in Gourmet Magazine for its sumptuous breakfasts.

Sea Crest by the Sea
19 Tuttle Avenue
Spring Lake, NJ 07762
(908) 449-9031

Rooms: 12

Someone once said about this inn: lovingly restored Queen Anne Victorian for ladies and gents on seaside holiday. Ocean views, fireplaces, feather beds, buttermilk scones, and afternoon tea—it offers an atmosphere to soothe body and soul.

Seven Sisters Inn
820 Southeast Fort King Street
Ocala, FL 34471
(904) 867-1170

Rooms: 7

The innkeepers, airline pilots, are full of life and reflect that zest in the decor and food. Seven Sisters Inn is an outstanding Florida B & B.

Trail's End—A Country Inn
Smith Road
Wilmington, VT 05363
(802) 464-2727

Rooms: 14

Nestled at the end of a New England country road, this cozy inn is a welcomed respite for weary travelers.

The White Oak Inn
29683 Walhonding (S.R. 715)
Danville, OH 43014
(614) 599-6107

Rooms: 10

Country pleasures abound at this secluded Ohio farmhouse—one of my Midwest favorites. Guests can participate in on-site archeological digs or relax on the inn's front porch swings.

Index

A

American Chocolate Week, date of, 4

B

Beverage(s), Chocolate Mudslide Drink, 87, 89

Biscotti, 34–35

Black Forest Cobbler, 42–43

Blackhawk Chocolate Trail, 31

Bran Muffins with Chocolate Filling, 16–17

Bread

Black Jack Muffins, 14

Bran Muffins with Chocolate Filling, 16–17

Chocolate Carrot Bread, 36–37

Chocolate Pecan Bread with Bourbon-Streusel Topping, 21, 23

chocolate spread on, 56

Cocoa-Nut Bread with Chocolate Honey Butter, 12–13

Sourdough Pain au Chocolat, 8–9

Breakfast

Black Jack Muffins, 14

Bran Muffins with Chocolate Filling, 16–17

Chocolate Breakfast Taco, 11

Chocolate Honey Soufflé, 24–25

Chocolate Mint Breakfast Chews, 26–27

Chocolate Pecan Bread with Bourbon-Streusel Topping, 21, 23

Chocolate and Strawberry Crêpes, 3, 5

Chocolate Waffles with Cherry Sauce, 6–7

Cocoa-Nut Bread with Chocolate Honey Butter, 12–13

oatmeal with chocolate, 19

Sourdough Pain au Chocolat, 8–9

Brownies, gourmandising, 25

C

Cake

Chocolate-Truffle Cheesecake with Raspberry Sauce, 72–73

Cocoa Kahlua Cake with Chocolate Glaze, 75–76

Cream-Filled Chocolate and Raspberry Cupcakes, 55–57

Flourless Chocolate Cake with Fruit Purée, 79

Mini-Devil Cheesecakes, 84–83

Mocha Bourbon Pound Cake with Cream Cheese Icing and Fresh Blackberries, 80–81

Old-Fashioned Fudge Cake with Walnuts, 52

Caramel Apple-and-Oat Squares, 31, 33

Cheese, cream, chocolate spread made with, 58

Chocolate

coating or paraffin for, 85

curls, 98

easy recipe for the pillow, 68

in a main course, 27

melting, 75

memories of, xi–xiii

pancakes, 96

storing, 39

Chocolate Bavarian, 99

Chocolate Breakfast Taco, 11

Chocolate Carrot Bread, 36–37

Chocolate Honey Soufflé, 24–25

Chocolate Jammin' Tassies, 100–101

Chocolate Mint Breakfast Chews, 26–27

Chocolate Mudslide Drink, 87, 89

Chocolate Pecan Bread with Bourbon-Streusel Topping, 21, 23

Chocolate Raspberry Cordials, 86

Chocolate and Strawberry Crêpes, 3, 5

Chocolate Waffles with Cherry Sauce, 6–7

Chocolate-Dipped Maplenut Creams, 93

Chocolate-Truffle Cheesecake with Raspberry Sauce, 72–73

Cocoa Kahlua Cake with

Chocolate Glaze, 75–76
Cocoa powder, do not substitute
    drink mixes for, 88
Cocoa-Nut Bread with
    Chocolate Honey Butter,
    12–13
Coffee
    Iced Coffee Cappuccino, 63
    Mocha Bourbon Pound Cake
        with Cream Cheese Icing
        and Fresh Blackberries,
        80–81
    Mocha Squares with Coffee
        Sauce, 50–51
Cookies
    Chocolate Jammin' Tassies,
        100–101
    Kissed by a Bonbon, 91
Cordials, Chocolate Raspberry,
    86
Cream-Filled Chocolate and
    Raspberry Cupcakes, 55, 57
Crème de Mocha Custard Pots,
    68–69

D
Desserts, chocolate are the cook's
    savior, 32

F
Flourless Chocolate Cake with
    Fruit Purée, 79
Fondue, Peanut Butter and
    Chocolate Strawberry Fondue,
    67

Fruits, Marbled Chocolate, 45
Fudge, served to guests to give
    energized start, 13
Fudge Pie, 38–39

I
Iced Chocolate Cappuccino, 63
Inns
    directory, 103–109
    (page numbers in italics refer to
        directory listing)
    recipes from
        Angel of the Sea, 84–85, *104*
        Asa Ransom House, 40–41,
            58–59, *104*
        Blue Harbor House, 11, *104*
        A Cambridge House, 3, 5,
            97, *104*
        The Checkerberry Inn, 71,
            105
        Durham House, 62, *105*
        The Fairmount, 79, *105*
        Flying M Ranch, 80–81, *105*
        Gail Greco's kitchen, 6–7,
            52, 67, 91
        Garth Woodside Mansion,
            100–101, *106*
        Gingerbread Mansion Inn,
            34–35, 93, 94, *106*
        The Inn at Buckeystown,
            24–25, 26–27, *106*
        The Inn at Cedar Falls,
            47–48, *107*
        Inn at Maplewood Farm,
            8–9, 87, 89, *107*

Manor House Inn, 12–13,
    107
Maplewood Inn, 16–17, *105*
Pinehill B&B, 14, 31, 33,
    36–37, 42–43, 65, *107*
Rowell's Inn, 72–73, *108*
Sampson Eagon Inn, 21, 23,
    75–76, *108*
Sea Crest by the Sea, 86, *108*
Seven Sisters Inn, 45, 50–51,
    68–69, *108*
Trail's End, 38–39, *109*
White Oak Inn, 99, *109*

K
Kahlua Chocolate Truffles, 97
Kissed by a Bonbon, 91

M
Marbled Chocolate Fruits, 45
Mini-Devil Cheesecakes, 84–83
Mints on the Pillow, 94
Mocha Bourbon Pound Cake
    with Cream Cheese Icing and
    Fresh
Blackberries, 80–81
Mocha Squares with Coffee
    Sauce, 50–51

O
Oatmeal, with chocolate, 19
Old-Fashioned Fudge Cake
    with Walnuts, 52
Orange Chocolate Biscotti with
    Chocolate Glaze, 34–35

Orange-Walnut Chocolate Tart,
47–48

P
Pancakes, chocolate, 96
Paraffin, suggested for chocolate
left out all day, 83
Peanut Butter and Chocolate
Strawberry Fondue, 67
Peanut Butter Pie with
Chocolate Glaze, 40–41
Peppermint Parfaits with
Chocolate Sauce, 62

Pie
Black Forest Cobbler, 42–43
Fudge pie, 38–39
Orange-Walnut Chocolate
Tart, 47–48
Peanut Butter Pie with
Chocolate Glaze, 40–41

R
Raspberry Cream Puffs with
Chocolate Ganache, 58–59
Raspberry-Almond Paté, 65

T
Truffles, Kahlua Chocolate, 97

W
White Chocolate Fettuccine
with Strawberry Sauce, 71